D0364312

RENOIR:
PAINTINGS, DRAWINGS, LITHOGRAPHS
AND ETCHINGS

1. Portrait de l'artiste, 1915
Crayon, Private Collection

Renoir:
paintings, drawings, lithographs
and etchings

SELECTED AND INTRODUCED BY
NIGEL LAMBOURNE

THE FOLIO SOCIETY
LONDON 1965

Plates © S.P.A.D.E.M., Paris, 1965

Text © The Folio Society, London, 1965

PRINTED IN GREAT BRITAIN

Printed and bound by Jarrold & Sons Ltd, Norwich

Set in Monotype Garamond

Printed throughout by photo-lithography

Auguste Renoir
A Biographical Note and Introduction

The vast quantity of art journalism produced on the subject of French Impressionist painting during the last forty years has inevitably resulted in a plethora of dubious anecdote, misquotation, and uninformed critical appraisal. Renoir, in particular, has been a favourite subject for purple prose writers, some of whom, whilst professing to interpret the painter's vision, have more often obscured it as they watched the fascinating pattern of their own jargon unfold. On the other side, however, the excellent memoirs of his son Jean and those of the painter Albert André, among others, have done a great deal to clear the soggy miasma of romantic notion and half-truth.

Born in 1841, the son of a Limoges tailor, Renoir earned his own living from the end of his schooldays as a copyist decorator in a local china factory. The work was hack to a degree and it was followed by several similarly dreary activities—including the meticulous copying of appallingly sentimental images of devotional scenes from the Scriptures on to rolls of linen, as required by many Jesuit missions for their temporary chapels in the propagation of the faith overseas. Nevertheless, so exacting a task gave him a basic discipline in painting.

At the age of twenty-one, he had saved enough money to attend the École des Beaux-Arts in Paris. Here, his principal tutor, Charles Gleyre—a Swiss painter of a highly romantic nature but academic in taste—seemed to catch Renoir's imagination; perhaps the romance of Gleyre's earlier days in Egypt where he had lived with a Nubian girl gave some 'prestige' to the otherwise staid and orthodox maître.

Renoir remained in the Gleyre atelier for about eighteen months, almost until its close in 1864. His colleagues during this time were Monet, Sisley, and a young painter of considerable skill, Bazille—whom Renoir greatly admired and with whom he lived for a while in Montmartre. Later, in 1867, a brilliant portrait of Bazille at work was completed in a few sittings; in some ways it is among the finest of Renoir's male subjects and is included in this selection (pl. 4).

During the next five years he painted continuously. He is frequently quoted as saying: 'I never let a day go by without painting—or at least drawing.' A spell of military service in the cavalry during the Franco-Prussian War brought a brief interruption but he had already attracted the attention of several dealers, if only in speculative terms. Then, early in 1873, the famous dealer Durand-Ruel began to guarantee him a certain

measure of financial support; this association lasted for the remainder of Renoir's life. Durand-Ruel's gesture also encouraged the more timid collectors to take a serious interest in his work.

By 1876, when Renoir was thirty-five, he had already exhibited in the first and second highly controversial Impressionist Exhibitions. To appreciate how great the breakaway from conventional imagery was in these paintings is perhaps not easy today. But towards 1880, when Renoir was painting little girls almost entirely in tones of crimson and Prussian blue, the impact on Parisian collectors was as stunning as it would have been unthinkable for a London audience. Fortunately, there was a genuinely liberal bourgeois patronage with sufficient faith in its own judgement.

In 1879 came his marriage with Aline Charigot, a young girl of those full, sensuous proportions he idealized so frequently in later years. It was, as his son Jean has told us, a mutually warm and lasting relationship with no recriminations.

Renoir's loathing of artistic and literary fashions as well as the affectations of 'connoisseurs', never diminished. He was forthright, hearty or bawdy as the mood took him in denunciation of any form of sophistication. He was as bored by the fashionable trends in literature as he was by Flaubert's *Madame Bovary* or Baudelaire's *Fleurs du Mal*. After a recital of the latter, he remarked: 'I detest it . . . *and* all those females preening themselves and drivelling about it.'

Religious issues and dogma or feverish social debates left him unmoved; he refused to paint as a crusader in any 'cause' or make the least gesture of a social 'conscience'. 'When I paint, I never believe that I'm saving the Republic,' was a typical remark. Instead, for him there was an inexhaustibly luxuriant, constantly exciting world to be re-created every day as it appeared and dissolved in light, movement, and sonorous colour. Olive groves, red roses, anemones, peppers, children, dancing couples; no less, the frankly naked and sensuously heavy bodies of young girls (like the models Madeleine and Gabrielle) with their broad round faces—these images surged through and illuminated his world to the utter exclusion of the dissolute politics of Empire or Republic. He once noted down: 'An artist can do nothing if the person who asks him to produce work is blind. It is the eyes of the sensualist that I wish to open. . . .'

During the spring of 1881, Renoir and his wife left France and travelled through Italy where he painted happily and studied the work of 14th- and 15th-century Italians, Renaissance frescoes and, in Naples, the Roman designers. Although he returned to Italy in later years, it was the impact of this experience which both impressed and disturbed his imagery for a long time, and also contributed to the later crises of frustration in his development. Before they had reached France again from this trip, there came another kind of experience, an attack of the rheumatoid arthritis that was to increase its crippling hold with slow savagery until his death.

Whilst in Naples, Aline Renoir had modelled for a nude portrait study. This canvas (and a later version) remain two of the most intensely sensuous figure paintings of Renoir's before the turn of the century. As 'La Baigneuse Blonde' she sat in a small boat in the Bay of Naples—an opulent young body in the blazing light. It is difficult to assess the true significance of this Italian experience and a great deal of romantic nonsense has been written round it, yet the revelation of the Pompeian paintings, the dazzling light, and hard glitter of distant terrain in perfect detail—all contributed to the intensity of the struggle with his changing imagery. Certainly, there are very positive signs of a change—away from purely impressionistic terms—in 'La Baigneuse Blonde'. Often, however, this struggle was barely perceptible in his work, even up to the turn of the century, but it was revealed in many of Renoir's remarks and in the restlessness which took him to Algeria, frequently to the Midi (long sessions with Cézanne at Aix), to Spain, Holland, and yet always back to a house in Montmartre.

As the century drew to its close, Renoir's crippling arthritis took an ineluctable grip and the bitter northern winters of Paris were almost unbearable for him; he spent as much time as possible in the Midi. Cros de Cagnes, Grasse, and Menton with its protective screen of the Alpes-Maritimes, were also frequented, often with the entire family. At this time, the small ports were relatively free of even the Parisian tourists whom Renoir loathed: 'once outside Paris they spoil everything' was his comment.

His physical appearance now was startling in the extreme for those who met him for the first time. Emaciated, haggard, his right hand twisted even more grotesquely than the left (a cycling accident had fractured his right arm in 1897), and an intense muscular rheumatism now spread over his entire body. Until shortly before 1900, he attempted to fight off the inevitable by juggling exercises with pieces of wood and balls. It was useless. The fight to save his hands was already lost, and he returned to painting, accepting the incongruous, agonizing clamp-like grip which held the brushes.

To his bewilderment and some embarrassment, he was awarded the Légion d'honneur in 1900. Meeting his friend, Camille Pissarro, Renoir explained that he found himself undecided whether to accept or be boorish in declining. Pissarro jokingly suggested that it was worthless, as everyone had it. But he finally accepted, almost apologetically.

Financially, he was at last completely secure. He no longer took any interest in the new art associations. He was convinced that movements such as the 'Indépendants', created by Sisley, would be of no more assistance to young painters than the Beaux-Arts had been. This applied even to the Salon d'Automne which had originated as a tribute to Renoir's contribution to painting. Yet he was deeply moved when, in 1904, the Salon mounted a retrospective show in his honour.

In 1907, Renoir and his family were installed in the farmhouse of Les Collettes, overlooking the Cagne river. In this incredibly rich setting of orange trees and five-hundred-year-old olives, he was able to paint for long periods out of doors, and the entire property and terrain belonged to him for the rest of his life. Two skilful sculptors, Guino and Gimond, frequently came to assist and encourage him with his own sculpture. Somehow, he found the stamina to create, even in this physically exacting medium.

During the next ten years, he painted several hundred important works, although the daily routine became increasingly agonizing for him; it was necessary to be lifted into a wheel-chair each morning and his skeleton thin body was covered in sores which refused to heal. Aline Renoir died of diabetes in 1915 and he was utterly crushed by the loss of her ardent and loyal attachment. Yet the canvases were primed, the easel adjusted, and the lint bandages strapped to his hands for another day's work. 'It's intoxicating,' he would often say as he studied the model, or the olive trees in the morning light.

On the morning of his death, in 1919, he completed a painting of freshly gathered anemones. He was then seventy-eight.

List of Plates

Acknowledgements

The publishers wish to thank the following for permission to reproduce the works and for supplying material from which the reproductions have been made.

Basle, Mrs C. Delz-Roniger: 28
Boston, Massachusetts, Museum of Fine Arts: 23
Cambridge, Massachusetts, Fogg Art Museum: 37
Chicago, The Art Institute: 10, 17, 22, 34, 38, 41
Cleveland, Ohio, The Museum of Art: 2
Frankfurt, Städelsches Kunstinstitut: 16
Hartford, Connecticut, Wadsworth Atheneum: 39
London, Lady Aberconway: 15
   Lady Marks: 29
   Courtauld Institute Galleries: 9, 30
   Folio Society, Collectors' Corner: 48, 55, 56, 57, 58
   The Trustees of the National Gallery: 18, 19
Oslo, Nasjonalgalleriet: 26
Paris, Bibliothèque Nationale: 42, 44, 45, 46, 50, 51, 52, 53, 54, 59
   Durand-Ruel: 35, 36, 47, 49, 60, 61
   Philippe Gangnat: 24
   Louvre: 4, 5, 11, 12, 13, 14, 20, 31, 32, 33, 40
     (4, 13, 14 photographed by La Réunion des Musées Nationaux)
     (32, 33 photographed by Giraudon, Paris)
Philadelphia, Museum of Art: 25
Private Collection: 1
São Paulo, Museu de Arte: 7 (photographed by Giraudon, Paris)
Stockholm, Nationalmuseum: 3, 6
Vienna, Albertina: 43
Washington, D.C., National Gallery of Art: 8, 27
   The Phillips Collection: 21

Paintings

When one tries to assess paintings produced during a working lifetime of more than fifty years, there is a temptation to parcel them off into neat periods of development. But, as in all attempts at defining an infinitely complex emotional process, the conclusions are frequently inept and ridiculous.

This is certainly true in relation to Renoir's vast output, and to the several, intensely wretched crises he endured until as late as 1900. Regarding the inevitable movement away from 'impressionism', he said: 'I hardly knew where I was any longer; I felt as if I were drowning.' This particular crisis had lasted more than ten years, yet despite his doubts and his depression he had succeeded in producing such dazzling conceptions as 'La Yole', 'Le Déjeuner des Canotiers', and 'Place Pigalle'.

Intellectual considerations could never enter into the utter simplicity of his approach to painting; 'Men are too tense—they think too much' was a typical remark regarding his infinite preference for women as his models. The roots of much of his frustration (and even desperation at times) lay in the need continuously to experiment and extend the range of his technique, as is apparent in many of the paintings between 1890 and 1900.

Renoir was convinced that he possessed only a modest talent; that it must be developed at any cost to himself, physically and mentally. In the glow of a North African landscape or the glitter of sunlight on the smooth roundness of a woman's body—'La Baigneuse Blonde' for example—there remained the basic urge to enrich and amplify his deepest feelings by uniting mind and matter, to use his subjects, no matter how deceptively mundane they seemed, to express all that he knew and loved of the world about him. Something of his unpretentious nature is recalled in the remark that 'the business of pictures is to decorate walls, they must therefore be as rich as one can possibly make them'.

It is no exaggeration to call Renoir's struggle with technique, an obsession. The craft of the Renaissance Italians, the classical imagery of their designs disturbed him for many years. Their influence on several large works, including the monumental canvas, 'Les Grandes Baigneuses' of 1884, was uneasy. The didactic and intellectual examples of David and (more frequently) Ingres also led him into long and fruitless wandering in a 'neo-classical' atmosphere of hot-house aesthetics, and frequently altiloquence. But gradually he ceased to study the masters of 'sublime technique', and consciously began to sever all association with their example. The literary content and allegorical allusions behind much of the old masters' approach made him impatient. He neither believed in 'telling a story' with painting nor felt the need to do so. 'If you want to tell a story—take a pen and write it, or plant yourself in front of the drawing-room fire and tell it there.' Perhaps one of the few works that could suggest any narrative style is the 'Les Déjeuner à Berneval', with Pierre and Jean, yet one has only to compare it with most of the genre painting (particularly Flemish) of earlier centuries to appreciate something of Renoir's vision. To avoid even a breath of sentimentality and still produce the intimacy and warmth—the specific ambience of a family circle—reflects no less the stature of his personality.

However, among some of his contemporaries, Renoir's work was often bitterly criticized behind his back. Even Manet and the sarcastic Degas were disparaging from time to time.

Because of his hypersensitive nature, Renoir was inevitably hurt by the occasional outbursts of pique from those among whom he had worked and no less from the savagery of the critics. 'La Loge' received loud sneers from academic circles, many of the public and the art journalists. The dramatic power of this canvas is subtle; the interlocking patterns of shape and colour were a revelation to but a few—among them Durand-Ruel. At another time, it was suggested by an eminent amateur of the arts that Monsieur Renoir should be told, that 'A woman's torso is not a mass of rotting flesh covered in violet toned green spots . . . a corpse in the last stage of decay.' But sincere recognition continued to grow. 'La Danse à Bougival', painted late in 1883, not only marked another broadening of imagery but also caught the imagination of an audience who responded intelligently to the glow of a typically national Sunday scene in the provinces. It is important to compare the growth of this work from the style of 'Le Moulin de la Galette', painted some seven years earlier.

Although there have always been numerous references to Renoir as a colourist—particularly among his modern biographers—there is less reference to the man as a sensualist. Instead, he is frequently shown as someone between an ascetic and a Rabelaisian libertine.

Whilst those full-dimpled bodies of his favourite models, reflecting the splintering light, were both challenge and seduction, the infinitely disciplined physical response of pulling the brush across the canvas meant being utterly involved in the re-creation of a highly personal microcosm—the reflection of a living, trembling world of all the senses, all at once. It may have been a red pepper, a rose, fruit, children, no less than his beloved Gabrielle with her full peasant mouth and breasts—they all became the starting-point of an equally sensuous exploration. And he was incapable of imagining life without painting; it would have been an existence without touch, smell, or taste—as well as sight.

Renoir's impatience with those who were unable to appreciate the wonder of the senses, is typified in a remark to a dull-witted journalist who had been looking at the painter's twisted hands and then at a large canvas of a nude bather. The journalist clumsily asked how Renoir could possibly paint. 'Avec mon "chibre"', came the reply. That the genitalia do play their part in the plexus of a creative act as sensuous as painting, must be accepted by even the most squeamish. Certainly, Jean Renoir considers his father's remark an affirmation of the delight in the senses that permeated so much of his work.

Many canvases of Renoir's last years at Les Collettes

are considered to be among his finest. The series of women bathing, the nudes of Madeleine and Gabrielle, and the 'La Toilette' (pl. 31) have a great breadth of treatment as well as an intensity of colour. Yet, not a few of these late figure paintings reflect an occasional despair; the swirling torsos and dimpling knees sometimes appear tired and repetitious, as if the painter were forcing both the scale of the work and the emotional content.

During the last three years of his life, it would be useless to pretend that the agonies of paralysis, hernia, unhealing sores, and almost permanent insomnia could not undermine the flesh and test the guts of even the toughest. Yet he wrestled, physically, against the on-slaught, and most of the time succeeded in mingling his whole identity with that of an image. One of his last self-portraits reveals very little of material concerns but rather, a quality of immanence—a hint of the serenity found in many late works of Rembrandt.

Technically, his application was as swift as ever. Long after he had ceased to walk and worked entirely from a wheel-chair, the entire concept of his design was touched in with broad abstract tones; these were transparently thin washes of colour diluted with turpentine. Next came the brightest values of the work, this time thickly painted; then finally, the whole picture was worked over in full colour and the transparency maintained by the use of oil and varnish as a medium. It was a variant of the 16th-century Venetian technique, and in this way Renoir achieved a richness of total effect as well as unity of colour.

'Painting is first of all a manual job and one must be a good workman' was a saying he often repeated and never contradicted in deed.

During his last years, artists with powerful imagery had began to build utterly different concepts to anything previously envisaged. Picasso, Matisse, Kandinsky were creating another kind of communication. Yet Renoir was able to sympathize with many of their aims and recognized the inevitability of such an upheaval. His own contribution had been made in full—'to create riches with modest means'.

2. Mademoiselle Romaine Lacaux, 1864
81 ×64.5 cm. Cleveland, Ohio, The Museum of Art, Gift of Hanna Fund

3. Le Cabaret de la Mère Anthony, 1866
193 ×130 cm. Stockholm, Nationalmuseum

4. Portrait de Bazille, 1867
103 × 73 cm. Paris, Louvre

5. Chalands sur la Seine, *c.* 1868
45.5 ×64 cm. Paris, Louvre

6. 'La Grenouillère', c. 1869
66 × 79 cm. Stockholm, Nationalmuseum

7. La Baigneuse au Griffon, 1870
184×115 cm. São Paulo, Museu de Arte

8. La Danseuse, 1874

142 × 94 cm. Washington, National Gallery of Art, Widener Collection

9. La Loge, 1874
   80 × 63.5 cm. London, Courtauld Institute Galleries

10. Au Cirque Fernando, 1875/6
    130 × 97.5 cm. Chicago, The Art Institute, Potter Palmer Collection

11. Femme nue en Plein Air, 1876
79 × 63.5 cm. Paris, Louvre

12. La Liseuse, *c.* 1876
45.5 × 38 cm. Paris, Louvre

13. Le Moulin de la Galette, 1876
130×172.5 cm. Paris, Louvre

14. Portrait de Madame Charpentier, *c.* 1877
45.5 × 38 cm. Paris, Louvre

15. La Yole, 1878
71×92 cm. London, Lady Aberconway Collection

16. La Fin du Déjeuner, 1879
99 × 81.5 cm. Frankfurt, Städelsches Kunstinstitut

17. La Brodeuse, 1879

61.5 × 50.5 cm. Chicago, The Art Institute, Mr and Mrs Lewis L. Coburn Memorial Collection

18. Les Parapluies, 1879
178 × 111.5 cm. London, National Gallery

19. La Première Sortie, 1880
   64.5 × 50 cm. London, National Gallery

22. Fruits du Midi, 1881
50.5 ×68 cm. Chicago, The Art Institute, Mr and Mrs Martin A. Ryerson Collection

23. La Danse à Bougival, 1883
178×95.5 cm. Boston, Massachusetts, Museum of Fine Arts

24. Madame Renoir et son Fils Pierre, *c.* 1885
   81 × 64.5 cm. Paris, Philippe Gangnat Collection

25. Les Grandes Baigneuses, 1884/7
115 × 167 cm. Philadelphia, Museum of Art, Tyson Collection

26. La Petite Baigneuse Blonde, *c.* 1887
60 × 53.5 cm. Oslo, Nasjonalgalleriet

27. Baigneuse se Coiffant, 1894
81 × 64.5 cm. Washington, National Gallery of Art, Chester Dale Collection

28. Gabrielle et Jean Renoir, 1895
Pastel, 59 × 45.5 cm. Basle, Mrs C. Delz-Roniger

29. Le Déjeuner à Berneval, 1898
   81 × 64.5 cm. London, Lady Marks Collection

30. Portrait d'Ambroise Vollard, 1908
80 × 54.5 cm. London, Courtauld Institute Galleries

31. La Toilette, 1910
55 ×45.5 cm. Paris, Louvre

32. Gabrielle à la Rose, 1911
     55 ×46 cm. Paris, Louvre

33. Femme en Bleu, 1913
    65 × 54 cm. Paris, Louvre

Drawings
Lithographs and
Etchings

At only one period was Renoir concerned with drawing as an end in itself. Many of these examples are now unquestionably lost and those remaining are frequently difficult to place in relation to his long working life.

It has, however, been possible to show in this selection some of the drawings which possess an almost austere linear discipline in violent contrast to the broad black and sanguine chalk effects of his latter years. The many attempts to explain or justify why one technique was used at one time and not at another, make tedious reading—and indeed it is perhaps nearly as fruitless as trying to offer a universal definition of 'drawing'.

Renoir has sometimes been credited with the accomplishment of marrying colour with line, which, to say the very least, is an ambiguous expression. Yet, for many years part of his dilemma was born of the despair he felt when faced with such a graphic dichotomy—the act of releasing an emotional image in linear or 'drawn' colour. Part of the problem seemed solved by Degas, but not for Renoir. As a draughtsman, he had an utterly different thought process, training, and reaction to his environment from most of his contemporaries, with the possible exception of Monet. Even here, one is tempted to question whether Monet's talent was of similar mould—as a draughtsman. They certainly shared common aims and beliefs as naturally as they ate their frugal bean and lentil soups together in the lean years after the Beaux-Arts studies, but that is probably as much as can be said in terms of an affinity in graphic outlook.

The discipline of linear drawing (of which several studies for 'Les Baigneuses' are typical examples) is one of the most exacting and sometimes stultifying techniques a painter can use. Renoir was not unaware of this. He referred to his several years of drawing study as 'Ingresque', not without some irony. He was also far more conscious than most painters of his time, that there existed a peculiarly immanent quality in drawing as a language in its own right.

Although few of his drawings can truthfully be considered as complete expressions of purpose in themselves, there exist a series of designs drawn specifically as Press work for a journal, La Vie Moderne. Renoir's brother Edmond was a member of the staff on this paper, which had a wide circulation in the 'eighties. The cover drawings at this time as well as some of the short story illustrations were by Renoir.

Lithography, line and soft ground etching attracted Renoir not merely as a graphic extension of his work as a painter but also as a challenge. Unfortunately, some of the print-making lacked the spontaneity of his original draughtsmanship. The prints, in fact, were frequently done from existing pen or chalk drawings and were not conceived as prints, drawn directly on to the plate or stone. And again, the proofing of the work was very often carried out for him. No doubt his increasing manual infirmity made this frequently necessary.

The wide range of softly merging tones which occur with careful etching in the soft ground process, pleased Renoir; the medium offered a multiplication of all the qualities in a free chalk drawing as well as allowing contrast with fine lines if required. Considered purely as prints, they are frequently more successful than the lithographs, although he fully appreciated the immense richness of effect which the stone allowed.

Baudelaire had written at length on the subject of drawing whilst Renoir was achieving some of his aims in painting during the 'seventies, and among the less specious opinions of the poet was the remark that 'drawing should be like Nature, living and restless'. This was an affirmation of much that the Impressionists held as part of their creed. But further. There could be no lines in Nature. Only iridescent masses of colour interacting one with another; contours could not exist, no form must be isolated from its environment. Renoir's break away from the sacred cow of Impressionist creed was irrevocable. His reaction had the effect of deliberately strapping himself into what Baudelaire called 'a linear straitjacket'. Yet, if the drawings of his later years are studied carefully, the lessons of linear definition and discipline are seen as an invaluable part of their roots; they exist in their own right, because of Renoir's determination to come to terms with essential spontaneity whilst curbing the excesses, the clutter of non-essentials.

He has seldom been considered as a draughtsman and since art lecturers and historians frequently appear obliged to discuss him in relation to Monet, Sisley, Cézanne, and Manet and their paintings, there often emerges an aura, a mystique which obscures Renoir's range and intention of expression. All too often, his highly individual approach is not fully appreciated because of this tendency to associate his draughtsmanship with the main body of Impressionists—few of whom made drawings of purely 'graphic' significance, and would in fact have probably derided such a notion.

Today, it is out of the question completely to redress the record of misapprehension and dubious interpretation since so many of the original drawings, the links in the chain of development, are lost. The work of Degas, for example, may be studied on a broad scale with confidence. But of all Renoir's contemporaries, he was possibly the only one who worked most of his life as a 'draughtsman/painter'.

Naturally, many drawings were destroyed by Renoir, deliberately, as a matter of course. He once remarked: 'It's silly to keep all that stuff. A dealer might try to sell them.' But again, many were also used, literally, to light the studio fire rather than use the morning newspaper. Thus it will always remain impossible either to assess how prolific a draughtsman he was, or, more important still, to appreciate his true stature as a graphic artist.

However, whether we choose to consider him as an innovator, or like Ingres who Baudelaire suggested was 'a colourist who had missed his calling', no amount of intellectual analysis or blind adoration of 'impressionism' can completely obscure the figure of Renoir as an artist of genuine humility and great humanity.

Much of those qualities is reflected in the graphic work still available to us. Perhaps in an age of negative values this should be more than enough in itself.

36. Baigneuse Marchant, 1883
Pencil, 295 × 195 mm. Paris, Durand-Ruel

37. La Rencontre, 1883
Pen and black chalk, 432 × 292 mm. Cambridge, Massachusetts, Fogg Art Museum,
Grenville L. Winthrop Bequest

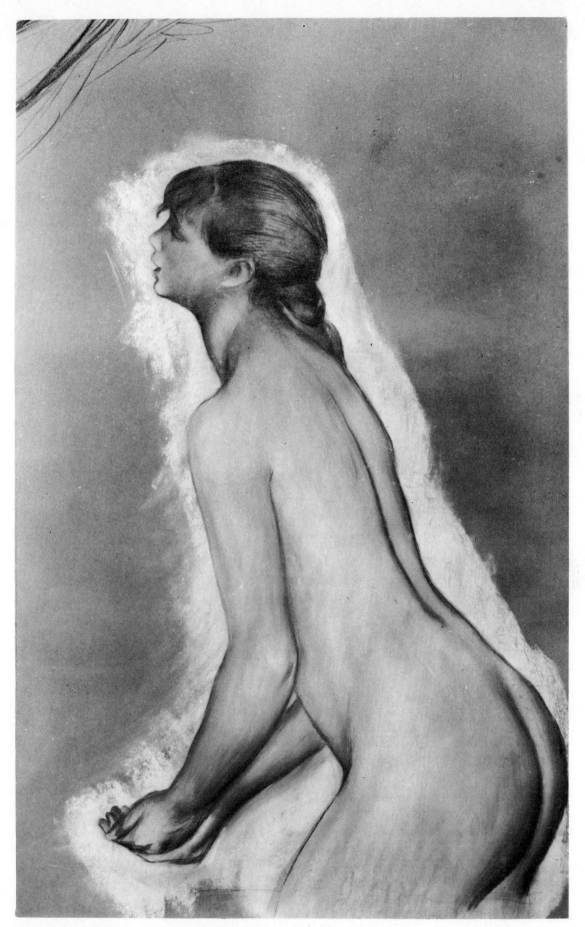

38. Study for 'Les Grandes Baigneuses', 1884/5
Pencil, 980 × 640 mm. Chicago, The Art Institute, Gift of Kate L. Brewster

39. Study for 'Les Grandes Baigneuses', 1884/5
Pencil, 238 × 352 mm. Hartford, Connecticut, Wadsworth Atheneum

40. Study for 'Les Grandes Baigneuses', 1884/5
Pencil, 105 × 162 mm. Paris, Louvre

41. La Baigneuse, *c.* 1885
Chalk, 425 × 311 mm. Chicago, The Art Institute, Gift of Mr Robert Allerton

42. La Danse à la Campagne, *c.* 1890
Etching, 220 × 138 mm. Paris, Bibliothèque Nationale

43. La Baigneuse, 1890
Pen and chalk, 300×185 mm. Vienna, Albertina

44. Femme avec un Seau, *c.* 1890
    Crayon, 359 × 238 mm. Paris, Bibliothèque Nationale

45. Jeune Femme en Buste, 1892
Lithograph, 532 × 403 mm. Paris, Bibliothèque Nationale

46. Les Deux Baigneuses, 1895
   Etching, 262 × 241 mm. Paris, Bibliothèque Nationale

47. Jeunes Filles Fleurissant leurs Chapeaux, 1892/3
Pastel, 595 × 455 mm. Paris, Durand-Ruel

48. Le Chapeau Épinglé, 1894
Etching, 80 × 115 mm. London, Folio Society,
Collectors' Corner

49. Pierre Renoir, 1896
Crayon, 300 × 260 mm. Paris, Durand-Ruel

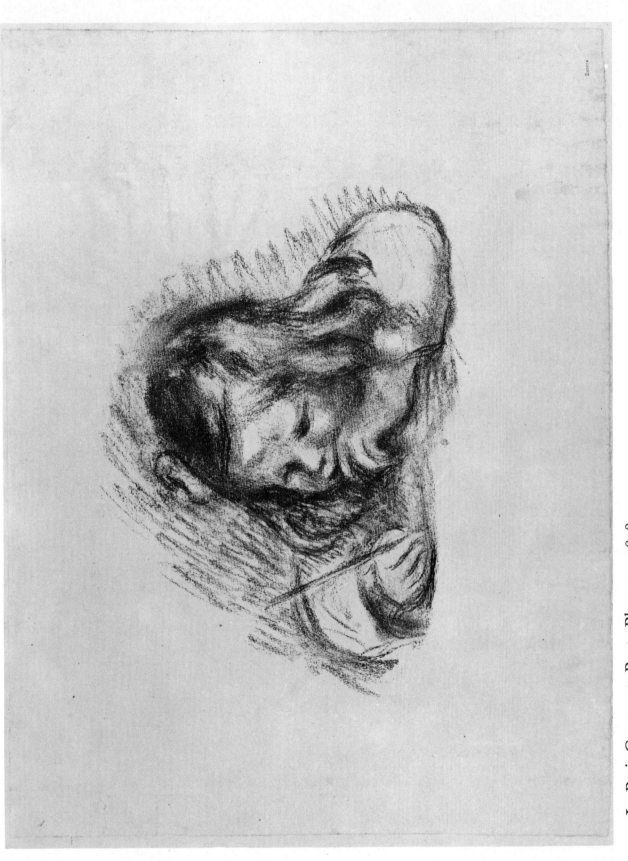

50. Le Petit Garçon au Porte-Plume, *c.* 1898
Lithograph, 398 × 298 mm. Paris, Bibliothèque Nationale

51. Enfants Jouant à la Balle, 1900
Lithograph, 600 × 510 mm. Paris, Bibliothèque Nationale

52. Auguste Rodin, *c.* 1902
   Lithograph, 400 × 385 mm. Paris, Bibliothèque Nationale

53. Étude de Femme Nue Assise, 1904
Lithograph, Paris, Bibliothèque Nationale

54. Baigneuse Assise, 1904
Lithograph, 190 × 163 mm. Paris, Bibliothèque Nationale

55. Portrait d'Ambroise Vollard, 1904
Lithograph, 252 × 330 mm. London, Folio Society, Collectors' Corner

LⅡ 39.

56. Étude d'une Enfant, 1904
   Lithograph, 248×330 mm. London, Folio Society, Collectors' Corner

57. Femme nue, couchée, 1908
Drypoint, 190 × 120 mm. London, Folio Society, Collectors' Corner

58. Femme nue, couchée, 1908
Etching, 190×130 mm. London, Folio Society, Collectors' Corner

59. Maternité, 1912
Lithograph, 540 × 480 mm. Paris, Bibliothèque Nationale

60. Femme nue s'essuyant, *c*. 1912
Crayon, 590 × 450 mm. Paris, Durand-Ruel

61. Portrait de Mademoiselle 'S', 1913
Crayon, 390 × 300 mm. Paris, Durand-Ruel